Are We Or Are We Not Saved?
The Once Saved Always Saved Dilemma!

Pamela S. Valerio

Copyright © 2010 Pamela S. Valerio
All rights reserved.
ISBN-13: 978-1456470364
ISBN-10: 1456470361

The Well A Church of Fellowship
"We Don't Preach We Teach!"
www.awtj.org * Email: wmcs123@yahoo.com

All rights reserved solely by the author. No part of this book may be reproduced in any form without the permission of the author.

Unless otherwise indicated, Bible quotations are from The King James 1611 Version.
The Word definitions are from Collins Gem Webster's Dictionary New Edition 2002, Harper Collins Publisher Great Britain.
Word study definitions derived from Strong's Exhaustive Concordance, Crusade Bible Publishing Nashville, TN 37209.
Theopedia online @ http://www.theopedia.com.
Bible Gate Way @ http://www.biblegateway.com

Take note that the name satan and related names are not capitalized. We choose not to acknowledge him, even to the point of violating grammatical rules.

Back cover photo by: Patricia Magilke
Excerpts by The Well A Church of Fellowship
Cover Image by IStock.com

Publisher Pamela S. Valerio

ARE WE OR ARE WE NOT SAVED?

DEDICATION

To the teachable spirit! The hardest thing to learn is what you believe you already know!

"But the natural man receiveth not the things of the Spirit of God: for they are foolishness unto him: neither can he know them, because they are spiritually discerned." (1Cor.2:14)

CONTENTS

	Letter	8
	Introduction	9
1	Meat for the Skeptic	12
2	Standing	26
3	A Life Cut Short	35
4	Your State	41
5	Walk it Out	45
6	The Vicious Cycle	50
7	Spirit Soul & Body	57
8	The Importance of Knowing	75

Dear Body of Christ,

Our salvation is not merited nor kept by the doing of the law. We are made free from the law by having the righteousness of Christ draped over us by faith through grace by His eternal work done on the Cross at Calvary.

We fail in all facets - He fails not. God sees Jesus when He looks at us and we are accepted in the Beloved, amen! We are justified by Jesus Christ upon our acceptance of Him!

There is a loss, but not in our salvation, but in our heavenly rewards when we sin. This, we must learn, so we can move forward in the security of our salvation.

Get well soon Church, the lost world is counting on us!

With much love,
Pastor Josue & Pamela S. Valerio

INTRODUCTION

In the body of Christ, some believe salvation is conditional, thus making their salvation dependent upon *works* and can be lost through individual sin or through unrepentant sin.

Through the teachings in this book, I pray that the Holy Spirit working through me will reveal that God's free gift of salvation, given through the grace of God, to each person, who sincerely receives Him, cannot be lost. Most know this topic as OSAS or once saved always saved. In God's grand and perfect design, did He potentially place conditions on Christ's work at Calvary? A condition so serious, that after you've given your heart to Christ, you are still doomed to go hell?

In my previous book, A Walk Toward Jesus, I briefly touched upon this subject, but felt God leading me into a deeper teaching to expound upon it. If some believers never grasp the birth of their faith concerning their **standing** with Christ Jesus, how can they expect to grow and mature in their walk with Him? If you constantly question your salvation, growth in Christ is put on the back burner, because you will never step out of the gate and activate the faith Christ gave you! You will be stuck at, "Am I really saved?"

Contrary to what you may currently believe, God made provision for the backslidden too. However, the journey they will endure will not be ideal, because as His Word states, chastisement awaits them!

In faith, we must believe, and understand correctly in that once we accept Jesus as our Lord and Savior, our **sin nature** was forever atoned for. What happens after that is up to you. You will either choose to become a dried vine that withers and dies quickly, from your **individual sins**, or a productive branch that bares the characteristics of Christ, and is spiritually maturing in Jesus' name, for God's glory.

Both branches are saved; the differences in the two will be in the reward department, because that is where we as believers gain or lose.

-1-
MEAT FOR THE SKEPTIC

Those who believe they can lose their salvation use John 15:1-8 to back up their belief. They believe the scripture *"Christ cuts off any branch that does not bear fruit"* as meaning, He would cast them away into hell. However, this scripture is not referencing our salvation; it is teaching about one's **spiritual state** not about one's **spiritual standing**.

Our spiritual state [sanctification process] is where we gain or lose in our rewards and our spiritual standing [justification], upon acceptance of Christ, is for eternity.

As we grow and mature in Christ, our fruit begins to mature and become evident. Eventually, that maturity allows us to begin to step out and walk in the gifts God has given us, and the calling upon our lives becomes activated and evidence follows us. The seeds are being planted, the water of the Word is springing forth your faith, it is productive, and the evidence of Christ is shining forth through you! Praise God! Even in the beginning, it may be small fruit, but just keep pressing forward in Christ.

Salvation **is not** dependent upon works, (Eph.2:9). Therefore, it is time to dig in the Word of God to uncover the truth it so richly provides to those who seek it out!

Beginning with John 15:1-8, along with other scriptures, we can walk this out to uncover the truth to see a picture unfold:

John 15:1 states:

"I am the true vine, and my Father is the husbandman."

1 Cor. 11:3 states:

"But I would have you know, that the head of every man is Christ; and the head of the woman is the man; and the head of Christ is God."

John 15:2-3 states:

"Every branch in me that beareth not fruit he taketh away: and every branch that beareth fruit, he purgeth it, that it may bring forth more fruit. Now ye are clean through the word which I have spoken unto you."

1 Peter 1:22 states:

"Seeing ye have purified your souls in obeying the truth through the Spirit unto unfeigned love of the brethren, see that ye love one another with a pure heart fervently":

Does **"taketh away"** in John 15:2 mean hell or early death? It is early death because you are being disobedient and not obeying the Word of God. In Strong's (#142) it means, *"to take from among the living, either by a natural death, or by violence; cause to cease."* Not hell here.

The word **"purgeth"** (#48) in John 15:2 means, *"cleansing through tribulation for growth and an expulsion of sinful ways."*

The word **"unfeigned"** (#505) in 1Peter 1:22 means *"undisguised, sincere."* In all things we are led to do, it must be done sincerely. As God looks at the heart of man, "....for the LORD seeth not as man seeth; for man looketh on the outward appearance, but the LORD looketh on the heart." (1 Samuel 16:7).

The word, *"unfeigned"* plays **a pivotal** role in OSAS and answers most, if not all, of the complex **what if** questions. For example, *"What if someone becomes an atheist after they professed Jesus?"* Okay, so what about those who are in this condition or backslide? Sincerity of the heart plays the key role here.

In Luke, we find a warning for those who backslide and/or do not repent.

Luke 12:45-46 says,

> **"But and if that servant say in his heart, My lord delayeth his coming; and shall begin to beat the menservants and maidens, and to eat and drink, and to be drunken; The lord of that servant will**

come in a day when he looketh not for him, and at an hour when he is not aware, and will cut him in sunder, and will appoint him his portion with the unbelievers."

It states they will be **like** the unbeliever who receives nothing, no rewards, but does not claim they are hell bound. In addition, take note, the sinner is still **called a servant of the Lord** and his sinful ways earn him something, but not hell. What does it earn him? The answer to this question is the premise of this book and will be answered thoroughly through this book. It will be up to the reader to read this book with their faith activated and have a teachable spirit.

Remember, we are only appointed so many days on this earth. We are instructed to store up heavenly treasures while on this earth, **"But lay up for yourselves treasures in heaven, where neither moth nor rust doth corrupt, and where thieves do not break through nor steal: For where your treasure is, there will your heart be also."** (Matthew 6:20-21).

John 15:4-8 states:

> "**Abide in me, and I in you. As the branch cannot bear fruit of itself, except it abide in the vine; no more can ye, except ye abide in me. I am the vine, ye are the branches: He that abideth in me, and I in him, the same bringeth forth much fruit: for without me ye can do nothing. If a man abide not in me, he is cast forth as a branch, and is withered; and men gather them, and cast them into the fire, and they are burned. If ye abide in me, and my words abide in you, ye shall ask what ye will, and it shall be done unto you. Herein is my Father glorified, that ye bear much fruit; so shall ye be my disciples.**"

Parts of these verses describe when a believer falls into willful sin. (We all sin and come short of the glory of God as shown in Romans 3:23). Therefore, this scripture should immediately begin to curve one's belief, toward believing, that one cannot lose their salvation. This is where belief and faith must become active in you. Because, if a person continues to believe that upon their confession for our Savior is conditional, the enemy will succeed in keeping that person a skeptic and possibly a babe in Christ. A babe that does not get to walk in their calling; a babe that loses so much of God working through their life! This could already be considered a huge loss of a reward, so to speak!

To believe a believer can lose their salvation, completely contradicts what the Bible tells us, how? Look what Ephesians 2:8-9 states, "For by grace you have been saved through faith and that not of yourselves; it is the gift of God, not of works, lest anyone should boast."

Is Christ someone Whom would take back a free gift, which is given by grace, to those who accepted it? No, because we do not gain favor from the Lord by our actions, [works] so how can we lose our salvation because of our actions, [works]? *We do not do good works to get saved; we do good works because we **ARE** saved!*

Works is not the litmus test for keeping our salvation. Because there is not a test we can take regarding our salvation, because it does not involve anything we pass or fail at. This is how God can say He is no respecter of persons and how He sees all His people the same. When you read the following verses, imagine standing ready before God, ready to do His commands. We are all the same right out of the gate!

Acts 10:33-35 states:

"Immediately therefore I sent to thee; and thou hast well done that thou art come. Now therefore are we all here present before God, to hear all things that are commanded thee of God. Then Peter opened his mouth, and said, of a truth I perceive that God is no respecter of persons: But in every nation he that feareth him, and worketh righteousness, is accepted with him."

Our salvation is solely dependent upon our belief in Christ Jesus and our acceptance of the work He did at Calvary. It is this simple! However, because of the many hardcore skeptics, we continue. Remember, the teachable spirit catches the truth. A hardcore self-believed keeps the devil's tale!

Upon salvation, Christ becomes our foundation and our **STANDING** becomes certain as we read in 1 Cor. 3:11, **"For other foundation can no man lay than that is laid, which is Jesus Christ."** Justification is solely the transference of the soul from damnation to salvation, which eternally changes our STANDING. After we accept Him, we then begin to build the condition of our **STATE** through the sanctification process, during our lifetime. If we choose to grow and mature in Christ, by dying to our self-daily, it will **drastically mature** our STATE. Our heavenly rewards [treasures] begin increasing. Sin, and do not repent, you lose some rewards and possibly earn yourself an early death, (Romans 6:23). Turn away from God, no increase in anything either. Remember though, He will never leave you nor forsake you.

The skeptic believes a saved person *"will not inherit the kingdom of God because of their unrepentant sin."* Our entrance into heaven is **NOT** anything we inherit. What does the Word say about our salvation? It is a free gift as Eph.2:8-9 state. A gift of grace cannot be earned. To work for something is to deserve it, and that would produce an obligation— a gift of a debt, as it were. That is why works destroy grace as seen in Romans 4:1-5 and Romans 11:5-6.

Anything we inherit is something that we are worthy of because we have met certain **qualifications** while here on earth. Anytime the Bible speaks of inheritance, inherit, or inheriting, it is speaking about being worthy of it. Our inheritance in Heaven will be determined by what is left after the fire burns our works, (1 Cor.3:15). We could never do enough good works to get to Heaven. Only trusting in Jesus' work at Calvary and the Blood of Jesus gives us our entrance into Heaven.

Once you became a Christian, did you also receive the magic ability that enabled you to stop sinning?

No, you just became aware of the fact that you are a sinner. Some believe that once you come to Christ, you are no longer a sinner saved by grace. *That's another story, oh vey!*

The Bible states in Mark 3:27 "No one can enter a strong man's house and plunder his goods, unless he first binds the strong man. And then he will plunder his house." The moment we become a Christian the Holy Spirit comes to dwell within our human spirit. He becomes our protection from the strong man, [the enemy]. Interpreted in this context, in the **synoptic gospels**, [the four gospels of Matthew, Mark, Luke, and John] where Jesus's accusers accuse Him of getting His power to exorcise demons by being in league with satan. The strong man represents satan, and the attacker represents Jesus. Jesus thus says that He could not perform exorcisms (represented by stealing the strong man's possessions, i.e. demonic spirits,) unless he was opposed to – and had defeated – satan (represented by binding up the strong man)

Does the devil have the power to expel the Spirit of God that dwells inside every believer? No! When we are sinful, the glory of God is made less evident through us, and will not shine as brightly [as evidently as] when sin is present in our lives.

> "I know that, whatsoever God doeth, it shall be for ever: nothing can be put to it, nor any thing taken from it: and God doeth it, that men should fear before him." (Eccl.3:14).

> "In whom ye also trusted, after that ye heard the word of truth, the gospel of your salvation: in whom also after that ye believed, ye were sealed with that Holy Spirit of promise, Which is the earnest of our inheritance until the redemption of the purchased possession, unto the praise of his glory." (Eph.1:13-14).

God gives us the Holy Spirit as a **pledge.** The word for pledge used here is, *"arrhabon"* (#728) which means *"a pledge of future blessings."* A pledge is a solemn, binding promise to do something and we can rest assured that God will do what He said He would do, and the transaction He has promised is **eternal**!

God gives all believers the Holy Spirit, as His promise, for the future blessings of heaven that waits for them. Once given, it is irrevocable, though through sinful actions of men, is made less evident as God's glory dims through the life of a sinful believer.

The conviction every believer feels [that still small voice] must not wane or be pushed to the side, because once conviction begins to decrease or be ignored, the enemy will attempt to replace it with condemnation, in a heartbeat!

Once condemnation takes root, it is extremely hard to cast it out if one's faith has not been established enough to overcome it. The feeling of condemnation in the believer is one tool the enemy uses to make the believer question their salvation.

The **only** condition in this entire contract is whether we will accept Christ as our Lord and Savior and sincerely mean it in our heart, because God will know the truth. It is never a question of whether you will ever be good enough, because Christ paid the price while we were still sinners. The question is will you believe you are Blood bought purchased by the Blood of Lamb for eternity?

-2-
STANDING

If the devil can get you to doubt your salvation, your walk with Christ will always be on shaky ground, and each time you miss the mark with God, you will always question whether you are still saved. One must believe that the work done at Calvary was **eternal.** [1]Eternal defined is, *"without beginning or end; everlasting; changeless."*

Your STANDING with Christ changes once you accept Him. What is standing? Standing is the **eternal transaction**, which transfers the soul from hell bound to salvation, upon **a truthful declaration** of Christ, for eternity, Praise God! We are Blood bought [Eph.1:13-14] and God does not give refunds!

---

[1]n190 Collins Gem: eternal –without beginning or end; everlasting; changeless.

Once we received Christ as our Lord and Savior, we become sons of God, which makes us heirs of God, and joint heirs with Christ. However, at times, we may walk away from Christ though His Word says in Psalms 94:14 **"For the LORD will not reject his people; he will never forsake his inheritance."**

Sure enough though, you have people who just use the name of God, as they do things in Jesus' name for their greedy purposes and not for the saving of their soul, though God knows who is rightfully His.

There are Christians who know for sure when asked the question, "Are you saved? They will immediately answer, "Yes, I am saved!" They know without any doubt and are not swayed by the doubt and unbelief of others.

There are Christians that are saved, but are not certain of their salvation. They base their salvation on works and their natural surroundings. Unbeknownst to them, they fail to separate the natural (intellect) from the spiritual on a continual basis. They do not understand "Not of works, lest any man should boast." (Eph. 2:9). They have a belief that their works, deeds, or actions can condemn them again.

"But to him that worketh not, but believeth on him that justifieth the ungodly, <u>his faith is counted for righteousness."</u> (Rom.4:5).

It's two simple acts of **believing** and **activating** the faith Christ gave you, "For God so loved the world, that he gave his only begotten Son, that whosoever believeth in him should not perish , but have everlasting life." (John 3:16).

Your standing in God does not shift based upon your present state. Once you received Christ as your Lord and Savior, you become sons of God, which makes you an heirs of God, and joint heirs with Christ as Psalms.94:14 states. Your life is "hidden in Christ," and regardless of what you go through, you are still sons of God.

Romans 8:17 says:

"The Spirit itself beareth witness with our spirit, (our human spirit) that we are the children of God: And if children, then

heirs; heirs of God, and joint-heirs with Christ; if so be that we suffer with him, that we may be also glorified together."

This is why, throughout scripture, the Word of God warns us that we will not be without suffering, but it does not affect who we are in Christ. Therefore, when bad things happen to those who love God, God's predestined purpose, in the end, can only manifest good results as Romans 8:28 states, **"And we know that all things work together for good to them that love God, to them who are the called according to his purpose."**

Now the question becomes, "If everything depends on what God has done by sending His Son, then what does it matter how we live?" Read what Romans 6:2 states, **"God forbid. How shall we, that are dead to sin, live any longer therein?"** We have died to the rule and reign of sin. Sin's reign came in by the first Adam and eternally atoned for by the last Adam, Jesus Christ. In Romans 5:21 it states, **"That as sin hath reigned unto death, even so might grace reign through righteousness unto eternal life by Jesus**

Christ our Lord." This is not a card-carrying license to sin, but God has given us assurance, of His predestined plan for our salvation is not altered by life's circumstances or our sinfulness.

Some mistakenly believe that when something goes wrong in their lives, they are hell bound once again. John 10:27-29, addresses this unbelief, **"My sheep hear my voice, and I know them, and they follow me: And I give unto them eternal life; and they shall never perish, neither shall any man pluck them out of my hand. My Father, which gave them me, is greater than all; and no man is able to pluck them out of my Father's hand."**

Just as the Blood gave you salvation, this same Blood keeps you saved. Jesus' shed Blood cleansed the **sin nature** of each person and upon acceptance of this, one is saved.

When one sins, the confession for a Savior is not required again, because the individual is already saved. From this point onward, we only need confess and repent from our **INDIVIDUAL SINS!**

Some believe that we are no longer capable of sinning because we are saved by grace, once we come to the Lord. That is not what the Word of God says at all. If our salvation were dependent upon our sinful nature, no one would ever be saved! Thank God, the work at Calvary covered our sin nature with Christ's Blood for eternity!

1 John 1:10 states:

"If we say that we have not sinned, we make him a liar, and his word is not in us."

John 8:7 states:

"...He that is without sin among you, let him first cast a stone at her."

Eph. 2:5 states:

"Even when we were dead in sins, hath quickened us together with Christ, (by grace ye are saved;"

Whether we have sinned or have un-confessed sin, all our deeds are a work, even that sin. Un-repentant sin eventually leads us to be chastised by God, not sent to hell.

Eccl.3:14 states:

> "I know that, whatsoever God doeth, it shall be for ever: nothing can be put to it, nor any thing taken from it: and God doeth it, that men should fear before him."

Ps.89:30-33 states:

> "If his children forsake my law, and walk not in my judgments; If they break my statutes, and keep not my commandments; Then will I visit their transgression with the rod, and their iniquity with stripes. Nevertheless my lovingkindness will I not utterly take from him, nor suffer my faithfulness to fail."

A useful credo my teacher uses is, "You had better have your funeral insurance paid up because it is going to get used sooner than later." It is not saying here that Jesus sends them to hell; He is saying that He does judge them accordingly to their sinful ways. If you are willfully sinning then your branch [life] is withering [dying] faster and your portion is a short life. The promise of seventy years plus so to live life to its fullest is cut off because of your continual sinful ways, **"The days of our years are threescore years and ten; and if by reason of strength they be fourscore years, yet is their strength labour and sorrow; for it is soon cut off, and we fly away." (Ps.90:10).**

If our salvation depended upon our works, then none of us would ever be good enough to qualify for salvation. **"Not of works, lest any man should boast." (Eph. 2:9).**

Therefore, in each case, withered vine or productive vine, God's plan was designed perfectly and it was designed an eternal plan and is unchanging and forever! There is **no room**, is this design, for a conditional salvation.

My first act toward salvation is to accept the free gift offered to me by God's grace and mercy. My part is to activate the faith Christ gave me and simply believe John 3:16.

Is my salvation dependent upon a continual process of doing good works? No! If I backslide, am

I placed back into the hell bound column again? No! Jesus getting on and off the cross each time I sin must be tiring for Him! No! His death was a one-time transaction for all those who sincerely believe in Him. Our acceptance of Christ Jesus, believing in Him and making Him Lord over our lives, is what we first need to activate, by faith, so we can then move on and begin to mature in Him! Amen.

-3-
A LIFE CUT SHORT
CHASTISEMENT NOT DAMNATION

My son asked me, "What if a person once proclaimed Jesus as their Lord and Savior now decided to become an atheist, what then, are they still saved?" That is the wrong question to be asking. Let's put the facts together and see why.

- ❖ God looks at the heart and knows who is His.
- ❖ If a person sincerely believes upon the work Christ did at Calvary then their salvation is **eternal.**
- ❖ We gain and lose in our rewards, not our salvation.

Therefore, the correct question should have been, "Mom, what does a person lose if they decide to become an atheist, **after** they have believed in the work

Christ did at Calvary?" Look at what 1 Kings 19:12 states:

"And after the earthquake a fire; but the LORD was not in the fire: and after the fire a still small voice." (1 Kings 19:12).

The still small voice of the LORD will always remain with that person wooing them back to His precepts. If they continue in their sinful ways, eventually it leads to chastisement by the LORD.

An example of what chastisement can look like is to look at Judas Iscariot. His choices brought on all the ensuing actions and because God gave us free will, his end was tragic and God's Word is shown as truth.

Judas Iscariot was one of the twelve original apostles of Jesus, and best known for betraying Jesus into the hands of the chief priests. Weighed down by condemnation, because of his act of betrayal, he ended up committing suicide. The condemnation was so great, that he could not see the truth to muster up the conviction to seek forgiveness. God's Word held true and he was cut off sooner than later as John 15:1-8 states.

Sitting at the table during the Last Supper, Jesus being Omniscient, knew that Judas was going to betray Him. Yet, Jesus still chose him to be an apostle, which was an act of love Jesus projected toward Judas. Judas had a progression of time to make the right choice. One cannot neglect the free will that God has given to everyone.

Judas chose incorrectly and it shows by his act of committing suicide [withered vine, cut off and cast away] and proves God's Word as true. The same holds true for us. We, have been given a portion of years to make the right choices, if we do; we will be blessed by years here on earth, then rewards when we get to Heaven.

"The fear of the LORD is the beginning of wisdom: and the knowledge of the holy is understanding. For by me thy days shall be multiplied, and the years of thy life shall be increased." (Prov.9:10-11).

Am I saying if you are truly saved you will never fall, sin, walk away, or decided you never believed in God to begin with? This is your choice and God, being

Omniscient, always knew your heart, even before He formed you in your mother's womb. He knows all truth and all fakery and knows our heart.

Christ never fails and He is the one who draws people to Him. Therefore, anyone He draws will have sincere faith and will never walk away. They may stop growing in their faith and knowledge of Christ and mistakenly call it "walking away." They may even never grow in their knowledge of Him, but their salvation is still sure.

God saved all of His people out of Egypt but did all of Israel make it to the Promised Land? No! Was it because they weren't true Israelites? No! Was it because they were not really saved out of Egypt in the first place? No! It was because of their disobedience, their life; [vine] was cut off, [short]. They died in the wilderness because of their sin and their life span was cut short along with a loss of rewards!

> **"Abide in me, and I in you. As the branch cannot bear fruit of itself, except it abide in the vine; no more can ye, except ye abide in me. I am the vine, ye are the branches: He that abideth in me, and I in**

him, the same bringeth forth much fruit: for without me ye can do nothing. If a man abide not in me, he is cast forth as a branch, and is withered; and men gather them, and cast them into the fire, and they are burned." (John15:4-8).

You have to ask yourself, "Would Jesus dangle salvation in front of me, and I bite the carrot, accept Jesus with all my heart just so I could be sent to hell for a sinful act?" No, unrepentant sin will be burned as wood, hay, and stubble on my day of judgment, and I will suffer a loss of rewards Christ had intended for me to have. As well, if I remain disobedient by being sinful, my life will be cut short, not sent to hell.

THE SINCERE PROFESSION

Romans 10:8-11 says:

"But what saith it? The word is nigh thee, even in thy mouth, and in thy heart: that is, the word of faith, which we preach; That if thou shalt confess with thy mouth the Lord Jesus, and shalt believe in thine heart that God hath raised him from the

dead, thou shalt be saved. For with the heart man believeth unto righteousness; and with the mouth confession is made unto salvation. For the scripture saith, Whosoever believeth on him shall not be ashamed." (Rom.10:8-11).

Even in thy mouth, in thy heart, the word of faith, if thou shalt confess with thy mouth the Lord Jesus, and shalt believe in thine heart, thou shalt be saved. For with the heart man believed unto righteousness; and with the mouth confession is made unto salvation. It cannot be any clearer than this!

You must believe it in faith to receive it, once you do, your profession is sincere and true, and no one can pluck it from you. Thank you Jesus, praise God Amen.

-4-
YOUR STATE
NOT THE ONE YOU LIVE IN

Your STATE determines what's gained or lost in the reward department. This is what changes and it is imperative that we get this right because our rewards depend on it! Therefore, a Christian who willfully sins, will get into Heaven, but will not rule and reign with Christ.

Since we know for certain that the Lord knows who is His and if we are His, we can move forward with certainty, without looking back to question ourselves on whether or not if we are saved. God designed his grand plan so that we cannot mess it up. Praise God! We should continually look forward and examine our state daily!

"Nevertheless the foundation of God standeth sure, having this seal, The Lord knoweth them that are his. And, let every

one that nameth the name of Christ depart from iniquity." (2 Timothy 2:19)

Your STANDING in God is sure, but it is your STATE that can often vary due to the two natures that now exist inside of you. The old nature does not cease to exist after salvation, but you can overcome him. As the old nature continues to challenge the values and growing Christ characteristics of the new man, spiritual warfare becomes an eminent part of the believer's life in order to maintain focus and vigilance in God.

"For that which I do I allow not: for what I would, that do I not; but what I hate, that do I. If then I do that which I would not, I consent unto the law that it is good. Now then it is no more I that do it, but sin that dwelleth in me." (Rom.7:15-17).

Just like Paul, we often find ourselves doing things that we know are wrong and hate doing, yet somehow find our flesh engaged in doing. It is not the spirit that causes us to act out those things that we know are wrong, but it is the old man, the flesh, and the sinful nature that dwells in us.

This nature will never cease to tempt you, but this does not mean that you have to continue giving into it. You hold the power to overcome and conquer those things, which are tirelessly attempting to control and conquer you.

The saved know it and enjoy the fruits of the Promised Land. The saved, but not sure of their salvation often wander about in the wilderness, struggling with the old man on whether or not to return to the bondage of Egypt—the world.

The unsaved, but think they are, are those who refuse to leave Egypt, but occasionally join in with those who have been freed from bondage, for their own greedy purposes only known to them.

Here is where the catch-22, so to speak, comes into play. Those who do not believe in OSAS do not make the distinction between **sin nature** and **individual sins**. They lump the work at Calvary and daily repentance together and don't recognize that Christ atoned for the sin nature for eternity and that from here on out, we only need to "daily foot wash," repent. For those who don't repent, chastisement awaits.

The eternal nature of Christ comes in to dwell in the [human] spirit, (Gal.4:6), upon acceptance of Christ and His eternal work, thus forms the creature in Christ Jesus and the Blood atoned for the sinful nature of man for eternity.

When we commit individual sins, unrepentant or not, we do not lose our salvation. We gain and lose heavenly rewards. You really have to ask yourself, "Do I really want to run the risk of losing something God has waiting for me for eternity just to enjoy some sinful action here on this rotting earth, for a brief moment?

Adam and Eve couldn't even pass up a temptation and neither can we at times, which is why God's plan is perfect and when the work that was perform at Calvary, was for eternity. Praise God and thank You Jesus!

-5-
WALK IT OUT! SPIRITUAL VERSUS SPIRITUAL

An exercise the scriptures teach, concerning the spiritual issues, such as the topic in this book, is to compare spiritual with spiritual.

"Which things also we speak, not in the words which man's wisdom teacheth, but which the Holy Ghost teacheth; comparing spiritual things with spiritual." (1 Cor. 2:13).

Christ came as was promised in the likeness of sinful flesh, to condemn sin in His flesh on the cross. He took upon His body the sins of the world and atonement thereof was for eternity. He was buried and rose again on the third day. Through His death, burial and resurrection he atoned for the sinful nature of man for eternity.

God, while Christ was reconciling the world unto Himself, not imputing their sins and trespasses unto them, had imputed them unto His Son, Jesus Christ. Christ was the Lamb that was slain, having all sin transferred to Him, to take away the sin of the world.

If we believe this gospel by confessing the Lord Jesus Christ with our mouth and in our heart, believe that God raised Him from the dead we shall not perish but have everlasting life, sincerely, we are forever saved.

THE OTHER SIDE of the COIN

Now let's compare that to the understanding that we can lose or do something to forfeit the salvation of everlasting life that was promised once we sincerely believed.

The premise of the gospel is based upon the justice of God that needed all sin to be judged. It would take the Blood of a sinless and spotless human sacrifice, offered to God, for sin to be judged and to meet the just demand of a Holy God.

Man had nothing to do with the plan of God that was executed to judge the sin of man to redeem him from his sin. It was executed without sinful man being involved in any aspect. God, through God's Son, to redeem man from all sin and be justified to receive God's righteousness by faith, appropriated God's redemption for man. Anything that God did for man could only be received by man though faith, in what God had done for man through Christ.

All the work of God's plan, that provided redemption to man, was executed by God's Son without any work on man's part, thus making redemption God's complete and total work and not man's.

Man's part is to believe and receive what God has provided through His Son, Jesus Christ. However, when man believes by faith, man has nothing to do with the salvation that God provides to him by [2]imputation. It has to be by imputation because it has nothing to do with man being qualified, in any way,

---

[2] Theopedia online **Imputation** - our sins are imputed to Christ, i.e., he assumed our 'law-place,' undertook to answer the demands of justice for our sins.

to receive it other than being a sinner in need of salvation. That salvation puts us in Christ and seals us with the Holy Spirit, and no man can pluck us out of God's hand (or handiwork) nor can satan remove it.

Because we are in Christ, God has given us to His Son. Jesus said that **all** the Father has given me, none of them are lost (John 17:12, 18:9) and no man can pluck them out of my hand nor my Father's hand (John 10:28, 29).

"For ye are dead, and your life is hid with Christ in God." (Col 3:3). This is a fixed position that is concealed and locked, AMEN! We have a double protection from the Father and the Son, which is sealed by the Holy Spirit. All this is provided by God's grace through faith.

Can man be expected by God to keep and not lose what God judicially provided by grace through faith, when man could not provide it for himself? If man could keep it, then it would not be by grace nor would it be received by faith. If that were true, man would lose it in a second the first time he failed. Again, God's design is perfect, even for us, a creation that even at its best is seen as filthy rags. **"But we are all as an unclean thing, and all our righteousnesses are as filthy rags; and we all do fade as a leaf; and our iniquities, like the wind, have taken us away."** (Isa.64:6).

Praise you Jesus, for all the goodness and mercy you have bestowed upon us! Thank you Jesus! Amen.

-6-
THE VICIOUS CYCLE OF "WHAT IF"

What I'm about to share, I was guilty of too. Praise God, He revealed the truth to me, and I now have rest and peace concerning my salvation.

Many believers are walking around in the vicious cycle of wonder and what if. I picture them with one foot nailed to the floor, while the other foot just walks them around in a circle, while they try to figure out if their still saved after they have missed the mark with God. If you don't pull the nail out of your foot, and leave the ground floor of basic faith, you'll never experience all that God has planned for you.

What is the ground floor of basic faith? Truly believing and being secure in the following scripture:

> **"For God so loved the world, that he gave his only begotten Son, that whosoever believeth in him should not perish, but have everlasting life." (John 3:16)**

This is the simplest of scripture, but way too many believers' profess it, but do not believe their profession sticks. This is the basic level of faith and the most important one, because all building blocks of faith, from this foundation, are built.

It is rather easy to see how one does not truly believe it because nowadays John 3:16 just rolls off a person tongue like water off a ducks back and lacks the activation of faith. John 3:16 has almost become just a motto for the religious folks and the power of it is almost becoming blasé. "Yep I've memorized John 3:16 and I can quote it at any time," very spiritual, huh? No, it just means you know a Scripture.

Know you are saved! Allow the power of the Holy Spirit to come in transform you and do not look back and question your salvation! Receive God's free gift in Jesus name! Walk toward Jesus with the confidence in Christ, not of yourself, and know that you are saved and now a co-heir with Him because He is worthy and made the way for you!

Now with your nailed pulled, it's time to increase in faith and believe in what the Word says about the confession of sins.

> **"When anyone becomes aware that they are guilty in any of these matters, they must confess in what way they have sinned." (Lev. 5:5)**
>
> **"Then I acknowledged my sin to you and did not cover up my iniquity. I said, "I will confess my transgressions to the LORD." And you forgave the guilt of my sin." (Ps. 32:5).**

Key verse:

> **"If we confess our sins, he is faithful and just and will forgive us our sins and purify us from all unrighteousness." (1 John 1:9).**

In Psalm 38:18 it says, "I confess my iniquity; I am troubled by my sin." Understanding the difference between conviction and condemnation is important.

Conviction and forgiveness merge and produces an increase in faith. Condemnation conflicts with troubled and leaves your foot nailed to the floor, and you seeking after salvation instead of forgiveness.

Yes, we should be striving to not willfully sin, though if we could stop sinning all together, Jesus would not have had to die on the Cross. If you willfully sin after you are saved, God will cut your branch short and cast you into an early death, especially after you have been made aware of your sins.

He will give you chance after chance, but one day, your chances will run out. I thank God for the mercy He bestowed upon me when I was willfully sinning. However, because I am saved, He showed His mercy upon me, I heard His voice wooing me back to Him and I responded!

I am **living proof** of what the Bible states in John 10:27 **"My sheep hear my voice, and I know them, and they follow me."** I am also **living proof** of what Ps. 89:30-33 states, "If his children forsake my law, and walk not in my judgments; If they break my statutes, and keep not my commandments; Then will I visit their transgression with the rod, and their iniquity with stripes. **" Nevertheless my lovingkindness will I not utterly take from him, nor suffer my faithfulness to fail."** (Ps.89:30-33).

Why it is so difficult for a believer to believe that God will chastise us for our sins, but will quickly believe He will send a believer to hell?

Often times, when the basic level of faith is not activated in a saved individual, their walk with Jesus does not often mature. They constantly ask themselves, "Am I really saved?" If a person never gets past this point, after accepting Christ, then one can see how maturity either never takes place or is extremely slow.

As for me, I was in the latter category. For many years, I constantly wondered and worried if I was saved. I always had Jesus on my mind, but I also knew at the time I was willfully sinning. I would profess Jesus as my Lord and Savior many times over the years, when in reality, I only needed to do it once and at the time I did not know I was actually shortening my life span.

Instead of growing in Christ at that time, I stayed in a perpetual state of wondering. Not only that, I was scared to death of dying and being sent to hell so I made sure to get in an occasional, "I believe in Jesus and what He did on the Cross," confession. It was a constant lingering thought that never left my mind back then.

Today, because I know I am saved, I no longer have a fear of being sent to hell. Now my confessions are my individual sins. My focus is now on storing up spiritual treasures, which are the rewards waiting for me when I get to Heaven.

Some people approach God as if He is some big meanie that punishes us and is unapproachable. I've heard it preached that some relate to God as they would relate to their own fathers. If you grew up with an overbearing and unapproachable father, you most likely, subconsciously though, will believe God is overbearing and unapproachable. It is from this skewed version of God that some people never go beyond their profession and stay in a perpetual state of questioning their salvation. Some believers with this skewed version of God even accept other beliefs, when it comes to getting into Heaven. It gives them a type of security, which they feel they didn't get while growing up. Way too many people believe that just being a good person and doing good works gets one into Heaven. It sounds loving and peaceable, but it is simply not the truth, according to the Word of God.

God wants us to have a reverent fear of Him, not a scary, cowering, spooky fear! The Bible states, **"The fear of the LORD is the beginning of wisdom…"** (Proverbs 9:10). **"For God hath not given us the spirit of fear; but of power, and of love, and of a sound mind."** (2 Tim. 1:7).

Let us reason with these two verses, increase in faith, and begin to move forward, in faith, in our walk toward Jesus, Amen!

-7-
SPIRIT SOUL & BODY
THE MOST IMPORANT ASPECT

"Which hope we have as an anchor of the soul, both sure and stedfast, and which entereth into that within the veil"; (Hebrews 6:19).

Next to God Himself, man must be the greatest mystery. For he was made in His image, **"And God said, Let us make man in our image, after our likeness: and let them have dominion over the fish of the sea, and over the fowl of the air, and over the cattle, and over all the earth, and over every creeping thing that creepeth upon the earth." (Gen.1:26).** The constitutional make up of man, is not a mystery, but is widely misunderstood.

Spirit and Soul

Aren't spirit and soul the same? No, they come from entirely different words in both Hebrew and Greek. The words for spirit in Hebrew are **"ruwach"** (#07307) and in the Greek is **"pneuma"** (#4151) which suggests a strong blast of wind. While the word soul in Hebrew is **"nephesh"** (#5315) and in the Greek is **"psuche"** (#5590) which suggest a gentle breath.

Often, the spirit and soul are seen contrasted as seen in the following Scriptures.

> **"And the very God of peace sanctify you wholly; and *I pray God* your whole spirit and soul and body be preserved blameless unto the coming of our Lord Jesus Christ." (1 Thess. 5:23).**
>
> **"For the word of God is quick, and powerful, and sharper than any twoedged sword, piercing even to the dividing asunder of soul and spirit, and of the joints and marrow, and is a discerner of the thoughts and intents of the heart." (Hebrews 4:12).**
>
> **"And Mary said, My soul doth magnify the Lord," (Luke 1:46).**

If the two words (spirit and soul) were synonymous then there would not be a difference between this corruptible body and the glorified incorruptible one. This is not the case and we see it in 1 Cor.15:44, "It is sown a natural (same word as 'soulish') body; it is raised a spiritual body."

In addition, the difference is seen in Christ's own ministry, **particularly in his death** where the **three parts** are divided. The body lying in the grave, the soul descending into "the lowest pit" of hell, and His Spirit, that He committed into the Father's hand, going into Paradise, **all at the same time.** Isa. 53:10-11; Ps. 88; Acts 2:27 are only a few of the verses about His soul in hell for us, it having become the sin offering for our sin nature. Then His Spirit is spoken about in Luke 23:43, **"Today shalt thou be with me in paradise,"** He told the dying thief.

There were ranks in paradise just as there were different cities of refuge in the Old Testament, themselves a picture of paradise. They had to abide in captivity in these cities until the death of the high priest and then they were liberated (Numbers 35).

God, Who is rich unto all that call upon Him, must have had many to call upon Him in deathbed repentance like the thief and when Noah's flood swept over them. It could be that they formed one of those compartments in paradise, for Christ's spirit went and ministered unto them as seen in the following Scripture.

"For Christ also hath once suffered for sins, the just for the unjust, that he might bring us to God, being put to death in the flesh, but quickened by the Spirit: By which also he went and preached unto the spirits in prison;" (1 Peter 3:18, 19).

Christ had to divide spirit, soul, and body on his death to fulfill the three different types He must fulfill in the Day of Atonement (Lev. 16). For **His body** must be the sin offering goat that shed its blood on the altar. **His soul** must be the scapegoat that carried the sin away into the lonely desert, where it died a lonely death. In addition, **His spirit** must be the High Priest part of Him that offered up these sacrifices. Literally **Hebrews 9:14**, speaking of Him as our High

Priest, says **"...Christ, who thru HIS eternal spirit offered himself without spot unto God..."**

The fact that His soul died for us too is seen in **Isaiah 53:9** where literally, **"deaths"** is in the plural, and the Word states, **"And he made his grave with the wicked, and with the rich in his death; because he had done no violence, neither was any deceit in his mouth."** What love! Praise God!

The body is world-conscious. The soul is self-conscious. The spirit (when such approach is not blocked by unbelief) is God-conscious. The Bible shows that there is the "carnal" (fleshly), "natural" (soulish), and "spiritual."

> **"But the natural man receiveth not the things of the Spirit of God: for they are foolishness unto him: neither can he know them, <u>because they are spiritually discerned.</u>" (1 Cor. 2:14).**

Does this leave the soul completely out of God's plan then? Not necessarily. For it is like a plot of ground. "Ye are God's **"husbandry"** (#1091) (1 Cor. 3:9). The natural underbrush was on it until it was tilled; then the seed - the Word in our case - was planted, and the rain - the Spirit – descends; and with the cultivation of the Cross in our lives, up comes a fragrant garden spot for God to dwell.

There are two words for **life** in the Bible. One means **natural life** and in Hebrew is it **"nephesh,"** and in the Greek, it is **"psuche."** The other is **eternal life**, in the Hebrew it is **"chayah"** (#2421) and in the Greek is **"zoe"** (#2222).

The physical body only has natural **"psuche"** life and the spirit only has, or is capable of having, **"zoe"** life. "And if Christ be in you, the body is dead because of sin; but the Spirit is life because of righteousness." (Romans 8:10).

There is no place, where the Bible says that the personal spirit either sins or goes to hell. It is always the immortal soul (Job 33:28, Isa. 38:17). As seen in Eccl. 12:7, the body goes back to the dust and the spirit goes back to the one Who gave it, God.

"Then shall the dust return to the earth as it was: and the spirit shall return unto God who gave it." (Eccl. 12:7).

"Spirit," like the word "flesh," has a dual meaning. Mostly it refers to one's attitude. An example is, "vexation of spirit," or "a good spirit." A contrast between the figurative and literal meaning is in 1 Cor. 5:5 (literal) and 2 Cor. 7:1 (figurative).

When God made man, He placed the personal spirit room within him to be reserved only for Himself. Not even demons enter the spirit room, "....Get thee behind me, Satan: thou art an offence unto me: for thou savourest not the things that be of God, but those that be of men." (Matt. 16:23).

God will not enter in unless requested and if He enters, He will embrace the whole "house" with His presence.

HEART SOUL MIND and STRENGH

"**....Thou shalt love the Lord thy God with all thy heart, and with all thy soul, and with all thy strength, and with all thy mind...**" (Luke 10:27; Matt. 22:37; Mark 12:30). We are to be so in love with God that we are as the burnt offering placed upon the altar (Lev. 1:3, 9). Its whole being, the **fat,**

"Their heart is as fat as grease; but I delight in thy law." (Ps. 119:70), inwards (soul), legs (strength) and head (mind) were offered.

The **HEART** is the center, and springboard of life's principles (including the laws of Romans chapters 6-8.)

The **SOUL** is the personality of one's life (one's unique will, intellect and emotions, his "ego" and its individual traits). The word often refers to individual persons ("eight souls saved..." 1 Peter 3:20). Notice that the soul has a set of five senses all its own, as seen in the rich man's soul in hell (Luke 16:23, 24). The soul has desire and basic drives (for security, attention, etc.). It is possessive in nature as seen in Luke 12:19 which states, **"And I will say to my soul, Soul, thou hast much goods laid up for many years; take thine ease, eat, drink, and be merry."**

While man has psychology, the study of the *psuche* or *soul*, he doesn't understand the sub-conscious part of man, which, besides including the deeper part of the soul, also includes the spirit. God offers the best study for He made man and has the ultimate knowledge of him.

The **MIND** consists of the faculties of life or life's practice. This particularly includes the five soul senses of conscience, memory, reason, imagination, and affection. In Eph. 4:17, "…..vanity of their mind' which means "uselessness of their mind." God counts this as a terrible sin. **"Dianoia"** (#1271) or 'mind" is a contraction of **"nous,"** (#3563) mind, will, and **"dia"** (#1223). This prefix denotes a channel of an act. Therefore, it should be "something thought thru," which would involve faculties.

The **STRENGTH** is the character produced by all the rest. It is life's product.

> **The heart is, like a treasure box, what one has.**
> **The soul is who he is.**
> **The mind is what he does.**
> **The strength is what is produced.**

The **heart** is compared to the earthly heart, it is likened to an "observatory or covered place" in (Job 38:36); the reins (Ps. 7:9, Rev. 2:23); the fat (because of its richness (Ps. 119:70, Lev. 1:18); a well (Prov. 20:5, John 4:14); breasts (Nah. 2:7); a treasure (Matt. 12:35); ground (Matt. 13:19); a dwelling place (Eph. 3:17); and a writing tablet (Heb. 8:10).

The **soul** is compared as a gentle breath (by its original words); a bird (Ps. 11:1; 124:7); the belly (Ps. 31:9; Prov. 26:22, "chambers of the belly" -- the soul has unlimited possibilities, chambers). It is like a panting hart, "deer" (Ps. 42:1); a weaned child (Ps. 131:2); a thirsty land (Ps. 143:6); a goat (Isa. 53:10); sheep (1 Pet. 2:25); and a ship (Heb. 6:19).

God is an excellent teacher, so He uses excellent object lessons, so I am not stretching if I compare the individual believer to the tabernacle (or temple) because repeatedly the scriptures do this as seen in (John 2:21, 1 Cor. 3:16, 2 Cor. 5:1-4, 2 Pet. 1:14). After all, the purpose of the tabernacle was to be a sanctuary for God to dwell within. So actually, it can picture whatever is His sanctuary, in the New Testament, which includes Christ and the Church.

The tabernacle is a trinity. There is the outer court, an oblong sanctified yard, with an east entrance. Within it is the tabernacle with its two rooms. The first (twice as large as the inner one) is called by Paul the <u>"sanctuary,"</u> while the foursquare inner room is the <u>"holy of holies"</u> (Heb. 9:2, 3).

The outer, earthly court would compare to our "outer man," the body. While the tabernacle building itself, being in the "heart" of the court, would, roughly speaking, be compared to our heart.

As stated, it has two rooms; the "inner man" of our heart consists of our soul, which is like the "sanctuary" room, and of our spirit, which is like the holy of holies. For in it only the high priest (type of Christ) could come.

In fact, he could only come on the annual Day of Atonement. Paul tells us that this represents a "once for all" event, "Neither by the blood of goats and calves, but by his own blood he entered in once into the holy place, having obtained eternal redemption for us." (Heb. 9:12). Christ dwells in the holy of holies of heaven, and also within His inner holies within us. By spirit, He can be both places.

Our "once for all" Day of Atonement was when He entered our hearts. Moreover, just as no flesh could work on that feast day, so neither could we for salvation, "Not of works lest any man should boast." (Eph. 2:9).

Three things in the holy of holies picture Christ in **our** spirit. Understand that one cannot build doctrines upon Old Testament types, but they are illustrations of New Testament truth. This is valid in (Rom. 15:4, 1 Cor. 10:11, Gal. 4:24, **Col. 2:17**, Heb. 10:1).

So what are these pictures of Christ? Firstly, we have seen the high priest picture Him. Secondly, the Ark of the Covenant pictures Him. Thirdly, within the pillar of cloud which rested over the mercy seat of the ark (Lev. 16:2) was the angel of the Lord which was Christ in the Old Testament (Ex. 14:19, Acts 27:23, 1 Cor. 10:4). **"A threefold cord is not**

quickly broken" (Ec. 4:12). God's love "cord" that binds our spirit with Him is a **threefold** one.

What practical truth can we apply from the above? Christ in us, like the high priest, has **once for all** given us, since our day of atonement, **a positional relationship.** The ark with its valuables picturing the riches of Christ available to us (mentioned in 1 Cor. 1:30) shows that Christ in us gives us **a provisional heir-ship.** (Our soul will have no lack if it will appropriate the hidden riches of Christ's wisdom, righteousness, sanctification, and redemption, pictured by the manna, Aaron's rod, the law, and the mercy seat). Thirdly, as pictured by the angel of God within the pillar of the Holy Spirit cloud, Christ in us, "the hope of glory," gives us **personal fellowship.**

Justification means "declared righteous" (declared signifies a legal, judicial sentence pronounced in our behalf, not an experience based on our feelings). However, we are responsible to cooperate, and walk daily with the high priest in our sanctuary or soul room. Daily the high priest walked with his sons -- it pictures a cross, incidentally -- as they placed on the daily sacrifice, and ministered to the sanctuary furniture, they trimmed the candlesticks, placed fresh incense on the altar of incense (not to be confused with the brass altar in the outer court), and weekly placed fresh bread on the table.

While justification, a finished work on Christ's part, is pictured by the inner holies ministry, sanctification, which means, "set apart" and "made clean," is pictured by the daily walk in the sanctuary room.

To be set apart involves a walk. If you are at one place and want to set yourself apart to another place, you ordinarily walk to it. While justification gives us eternal life, a permanent standing in the house of God, sanctification gives us an inheritance, something that is more than a gift (Rom. 6:23, Col 3:24, Acts 20:32, 26:18). It develops our state of growth.

There are five words incidentally, that denote stages of growth in God's family. They are **"nepios,"** which means "Babe in Christ," akin to birth through two years old, (Heb.5:12-13). The second one is "**paidion,**" which means one goes back and forth between the carnal mind and the spiritual mind, (Heb.6:1; Gal.5:15, 16). The next being a "**teknon,**" and in this stage, the flesh expresses itself and one must learn to crucify it. Also, usually translated as "little children." (Eph.4:14-15). The next stage is a "**huios**" or adolescent, and at this stage, we ask the Lord what we are to do and He leads us. We have to come to a place of leaning on the Lord and His revelation and not of our own understanding, (Romans 8:14-15). The last stage is a "**pater,**" and is the most wonderful of the five. The pater is the person who reveals spiritual understanding, AMEN! A spiritual father is only concerned about the spiritual needs of those around them. A spiritual father is about others and not about "me, me, and me." A pater is selfless not selfish, (1 Cor.4:15).

Around the table, they all have the same standing, but look at their different states.

We must qualify the statement that the high priest's holy of holies ministry, pictures justification.

For although that is true, yet there are three phases to sanctification, and one of them was incorporated into that justification. For we are sanctified by the blood -- set apart as for our standing. **"Sanctify them through thy truth: thy word is truth." (John 17:17**), and this is usually what generally is meant by sanctification. It sets us apart as far as our state is concerned.

Then, there is that of being sanctified by the Holy Spirit (Rom. 15:16), Who separates us apart as far as service is concerned. In the normal experience, this is when one, as in Acts, receives the Holy Spirit after salvation. (The Old Testament priests could not serve until the oil was placed on them), but by Christ's offering Himself for us, shedding His blood, and by our accepting this as the new birth.

"By the which will we are sanctified through the offering of the body of Jesus Christ once for all. For by one offering he hath perfected for ever them that are sanctified." (Heb. 10:10, 14).

I might add that it was not just our spirit that was sanctified once for all. For the high priest pictures a complete sanctification when he sprinkled not just the mercy seat but also the tabernacle and all the furniture therein, our complete being, judicially stands **"And ye are complete in him, which is the head of all principality and power:" (Col. 2:10).** Of course, once the high priest placed the oil also over all the tabernacle parts, picturing when we were baptized by the Spirit it was a complete baptism.

"Who delivered us from so great a death, and doth deliver: in whom we trust that He will yet deliver us." (2 Cor. 1:10).

Justification, sanctification, and glorification describe the three-fold deliverance. For we were delivered, once for all, from the eternal **penalty** of sin **"And to wait for his Son from heaven, whom he raised from the dead, even Jesus, which delivered us from the wrath to come."** (1 Thess. 1:10). This was justification, and it came by the Blood, which, of course, is the basis for it all.

We are being delivered from the **power** of sin (habits, temptations) through our daily holy walk; that is sanctification. However, one day we shall yet be delivered from the presence of sin; that will be glorification at His coming. Amen!

-8-
THE IMPORTANCE OF KNOWING IN SEASON OR OUT OF SEASON

While in the final proof reading stage of this book, it appeared complete. God had different plans. I was in a good discussion with a friend of mine concerning the Word of God. We have some vastly differing beliefs and rarely speak on those issues. In the midst of our conversation, he asked the following multi-level question:

- If you believe the entire Bible, then you believe when God said in Luke 6:27, "Love your enemies," right?

- lucifer is the enemy of God, right?

- Does God love His enemy lucifer?

> If God instructed you to love your enemies, then should you not then love lucifer too?

My first response was, "Of course God does not want us to love lucifer." Where his immediately response was, "But if God is pure love He cannot hate, therefore we cannot hate, even to the point of not having hate toward the devil." I then stated, "No, God was speaking about human beings, not angelic beings." He then stated, "No, the Bible does not specifically state human or angelic." No matter what I said to my friend, he kept replying, "No, the Word never stated that specifically," or "God said to love all your enemies and lucifer is an enemy of God."

As our conversation continued, a growing feeling of "being caught out of season" attempted to grow inside of me. I had to fight back feelings of defeat though I know I am not defeated, because Christ has given me victory through Him, Amen! Most Christians will recognize that his questions are contrary to what God's Word states, but most will not be ready with the correct reply. Because I am Christ minded and have my mind on those things of Christ, I was caught a bit off guard with his question.

The Lord used this moment in a twofold way with me. First as a teaching moment so I could fully comprehend how important being ready in season and out of season truly is, especially in this day and age. After much thought and prayer concerning this conversation, the Holy Spirit showed me God was answering a question I have pondered for some time now. The question I asked God occasionally was, "Lord, when Jesus was tempted by lucifer, while fasting forty days and forty nights, when lucifer tempted Him, Jesus responded with truth and effectively rebuked the devil, would I be equipped [ready] to do the same in a similar situation, and it be effective?" Sometimes, when our Father supplies the answer, we need to be humble enough to recognize our insufficiency because His response will bring you to your knees.

There are few scriptures in the Bible that can be taken literally. However, most scripture must be spiritually discerned and studied out for the **whole picture to be made evident.** God is a spirit and worshipped in spirit and truth. **John 4:24, "God [is] a Spirit: and they that worship him must worship [him] in spirit and in truth."** To know Him, you must seek Him in this manner!

Secondly, the word enemies in Luke 6:27, is referring to another person, not an angelic being and if my friend would have taken the time to do the work on his own, he would have seen this. The Greek word for enemies is **"exthrós"** #2190, which means, *"<u>describes a person</u> resolved to inflict harm."* Who exactly is the enemy of God? **"…whosoever therefore will be a friend of the world is the enemy of God."** (James 4:4). As one can see, a word study is extremely important. The word study reveals the truth and meaning of the scripture and corrects the wrong understanding of "No, the scripture didn't point out whether enemy is referring to a human or an angelic being" because we can see that it does. If a person will not accept the truth according to God's

Word, that will be their choice to refuse the truth. No one can force someone to believe as you believe.

Third, either one believes the entire Word of God, or one believes God's Word is akin to a cafeteria line where one can pick and choose what they want to believe, to fit themselves, which is setting up a god of one's own choosing, thus breaking the first Commandment, Ex. 20:3 **"Thou shalt have no other gods before me."** When a person sets up a god they can follow they can make this god as loving or as emotional as they want, while avoiding the truth that God does hate certain things.

After further study and research, I discovered my friend follows The Universalists belief. They believe things like, "God loves us all so much that He will save us all; or "God is love, and will not send anyone to hell." Universalists teach that God is so full of love that He simply cannot send anyone to hell because to do so would be against His infinite love. They believe God will forgive all, even those who openly reject Him and/or die cursing God.

The central belief, which distinguishes Christian Universalism from Christianity, is **Universal reconciliation**, which means *all will eventually be reconciled to God without exception, the penalty for sin is not everlasting, i.e. doctrines of everlasting damnation to hell and annihilationism* are rejected by Universalist. Also, Theosis which is "deification-consider someone to be a god" or "divinization-regarding someone as a deity" and the process of a worshiper becoming free of hamartia ("missing the mark"), being united with God, beginning in this life and later consummated in bodily resurrection. In 1899, the Universalist General Convention, later called the Universalist Church of America, adopted Five Principles/Beliefs. Theosis being adopted and later added to their statement of faith in 2007 by the Christian Universalist Association.

1. The belief in God.
2. Belief in Jesus Christ.
3. The immortality of the human soul.
4. The reality of sin.
5. Universal reconciliation.
6. Theosis (adopted in 2007).

GOD and HATE

Part of our conversation centered on whether or not God hates. What does the Word of God say about God and hate? I will touch on this subject just enough to show through Scripture that God does hate certain things. He detests evil, and it is evident in the following verses:

"These six things doth the LORD hate: yea, seven are an abomination unto him: A proud look, a lying tongue, and hands that shed innocent blood, An heart that deviseth wicked imaginations, feet that be swift in running to mischief, A false witness that speaketh lies, and he that soweth discord among brethren." (Prov. 6:16-19).

"All their wickedness is in Gilgal: for there I hated them: for the wickedness of their doings I will drive them out of mine house, I will love them no more: all their princes are revolters." (Hosea 9:15)

In addition, one must recognize that the characteristics of Christ and the characteristics of the devil are opposite of one another. The characteristics of Christ that a Christian should drape themselves in are found in Gal. 5:22-23 **"But the fruit of the Spirit is love, joy, peace, longsuffering, gentleness, goodness, faith, meekness, temperance: against such there is no law."** What does Christ do for you? Matthew 25:35-36 **"For I was an hungred, and ye gave me meat: I was thirsty, and ye gave me drink: I was a stranger, and ye took me in: Naked, and ye clothed me: I was sick, and ye visited me: I was in prison, and ye came unto me."**

The characteristics of the devil are found in Gal. 5:19-21 **"Now the works of the flesh are manifest, which are these; Adultery, fornication, uncleanness, lasciviousness, Idolatry, witchcraft, hatred, variance, emulations, wrath, strife, seditions, heresies, envyings, murders, drunkenness, revellings, and such like: of the which I tell you before, as I have also told you in time past, that they which do such things shall not** inherit the kingdom of God." What does the devil do to the unsaved and unknowledgeable? he will keep them blind, 2 Cor.4:4 **"In whom the god of this world hath blinded the minds of them which believe not, lest the light of the glorious gospel of Christ, who is the image of God, should shine unto them."** The devil sets you on a path to receive the wrath of God, John 3:36 **"He that believeth on the Son hath everlasting life: and he that believeth not the Son shall not see life; but the wrath of God abideth on him."** The unsaved bare the fruit of death, Romans 7:5 **"For when we were in the flesh, the motions of sins, which were by the law, did work in our members to bring forth fruit unto death."** "For the time past of our life may suffice us to have wrought the will of the Gentiles, when we walked in lasciviousness, lusts, excess of wine, revellings, banquetings, and abominable idolatries:" (1 Pet. 4:3).

> **"Mortify therefore your members which are upon the earth; fornication, uncleanness, inordinate affection, evil concupiscence, and**

covetousness, which is idolatry: For which things' sake the wrath of God cometh on the children of disobedience: In the which ye also walked some time, when ye lived in them." (Col. 3:5-7).

"But unto them that are contentious, and do not obey the truth, but obey unrighteousness, indignation and wrath, tribulation and anguish, upon every soul of man that doeth evil, of the Jew first, and also of the Gentile" (Rom. 2:8-9).

"Thorns and snares are in the way of the forward [disobedient]: he that doth keep his soul shall be far from them." (Prov. 22:5).

Therefore, to believe one should love the characteristics that make up the devil completely goes against the Lord Jesus Christ. In today's day and age, many people have made a god that suits their lifestyle, instead of allowing God to establish their life in Him. Not one person on this planet can re-design or change the divine order of Gods ordained plan and creation, not one! No matter how good a person is, no matter how many hungry they have fed, no matter how loving, no matter how humble a person may bow, if they have not accepted the work of Christ at Calvary and believe in Who He is, then all their work is just that, theirs and accounts for nothing. Again, we do not do good works to get saved; we do good works because we ARE saved! Ephesians 2:8-9 "For by grace are ye saved through faith; and that not of yourselves: it is the gift of God: Not of works, lest any man should boast."

It is up to each individual person to activate the faith Christ gave them so one can begin to believe what Christ has taught in totality, not picking and choosing just the good parts and casting aside all the others.

Remember, John 1:1-5 "In the beginning was the Word, and the Word was with God, and the Word was God. The same was in the beginning with God. All things were made by him; and without him was not anything made that was made. In him was life;

and the life was the light of men. And the light shineth in darkness; and the darkness comprehended it not."

John 3:17-21 "For God sent not his Son into the world to condemn the world; but that the world through him might be saved. He that believeth on him is not condemned: but he that believeth not is condemned already, because he hath not believed in the name of the only begotten Son of God. And this is the condemnation, that light is come into the world, and men loved darkness rather than light, because their deeds were evil. For every one that doeth evil hateth the light, neither cometh to the light, lest his deeds should be reproved. But he that doeth truth cometh to the light that his deeds may be made manifest, that they are wrought in God."

Gal 5:24-25 "And they that are Christ's have crucified the flesh with the affections and lusts. If we live in the Spirit, let us also walk in the Spirit." AMEN!

ABOUT THE AUTHOR

Pamela worked in the Photo Industry for 18 years, having also co-owned a 1 Hr. Photo lab from 1996-1998. In 2005, Pamela and her husband, Pastor Joshua Valerio Jr., founded The Well A Church of Fellowship after hearing the Lord impress on their hearts to build an outreach center in their community.

In the late 80's, Pamela began suffering from a panic and anxiety disorder. Having tried counseling and various medications to relieve the symptoms, nothing seemed too worked. In 1997, she began searching God for the answer. This search led her to begin writing a book entitled, "Who is the Bride of Christ." While in the process of writing this book, she suffered a life-altering injury that changed her course in life.

Having undergone lumbar surgery in 2003, enduring countless days of pain and physical therapy, Pamela fell into a deep period of asking God, why. She had a hard time understanding the answer to this question because she had been in intense biblical studies and saturating herself with the Lord at the time of this injury. The original search was to seek healing from the anxiety when this physical injury happened.

It was years later, through continued earnest seeking, she began to realize, if it had not been for God sending her through such a wilderness walk, she wouldn't have been given the rest of the story! Changing the title to "A Walk Toward Jesus" and completing the book in 2010, is victory. Pamela learned, through that trial, what must take place, before victory and freedom comes. "So many times we sit in church and only hear the message of victory, but we never hear the message of the wilderness and why we go through it.

Before her injury, Pamela was studying at the Temple Faith Based Institute. Completing her course study in Restoration Faith Based Counseling just mere weeks before her injury occurred. Writing has become a form of therapeutic exercise for Pamela, she says, *"Having always taken extensive notes while studying, I found a way to compile my notes into book form and pray that others can benefit from what I have to offer."*

ISBN-13: 978-1456470364
ISBN-10: 1456470361

Made in the USA
Charleston, SC
31 May 2011